See for Myself

Jaap Tuinman

CONSULTANTS
Anna Cresswell
Gail Heald-Taylor
Lynda Hodson
Glen Huser

ADVISER
Moira McKenzie

PROGRAMME EDITOR
Kathleen Doyle

Schofield & Sims Ltd
Educational Publishers

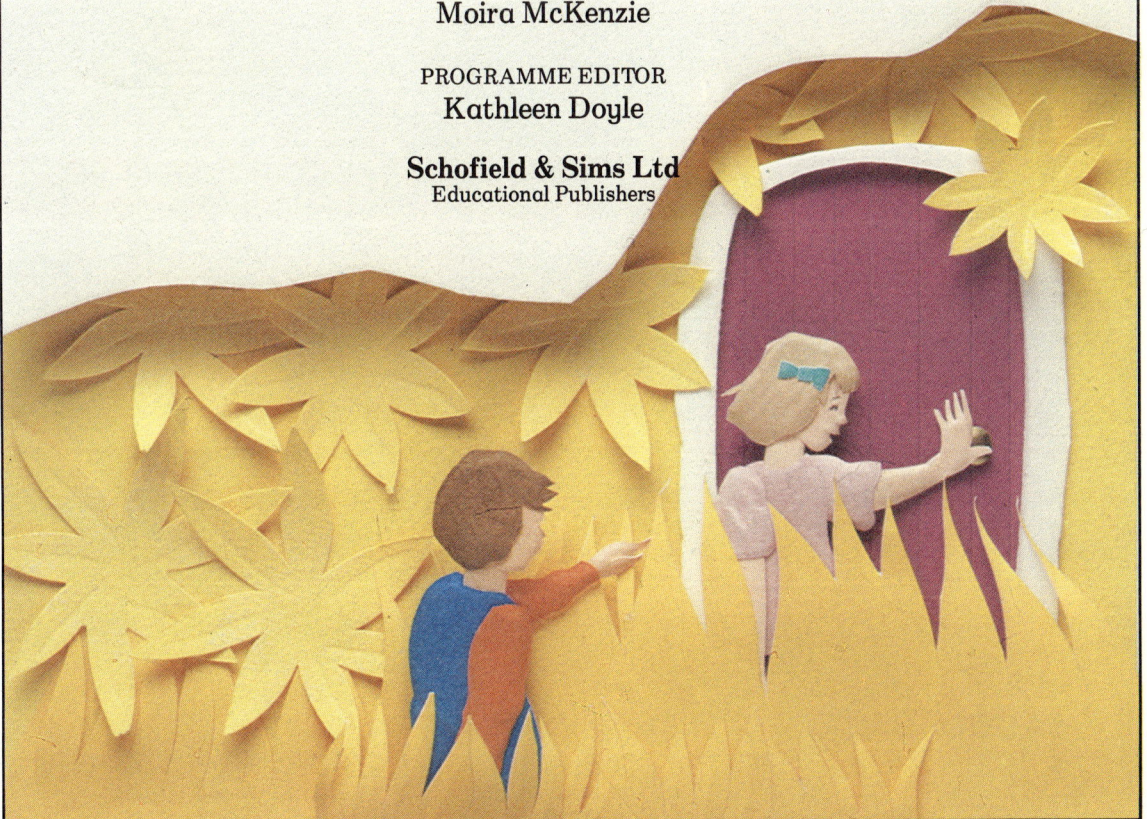

Journeys
Level Six
See for Myself

TEACHER CONTRIBUTORS
Barbara Currie
Jay Milne

ISBN 0-7217-0571-5

Printed and bound in England
ABCDEFGHIJ 9876543210

First printed 1985

2

ACKNOWLEDGEMENTS

For kind permission to reprint copyrighted material, acknowledgement is hereby made to the following:

Atheneum Publishers, Inc. for the poem "My Box." Myra Cohn Livingston, "My Box," in *The Way Things Are and Other Poems*. Copyright © 1974 by Myra Cohn Livingston. A Margaret K. McElderry Book. Reprinted with the permission of Atheneum Publishers.

ATV Music Group for the song "The Marvellous Toy" by Tom Paxton. © copyright 1961 Cherry Lane Music Publ. Co. Inc. Used by permission of Welbeck Music of Canada Corp. Toronto. All rights reserved.

Dial Books for Young Readers for the story "Secret Favour Day" from *Woodruff And The Clocks* by Elizabeth Bram.

Sibyl Hancock for *Mario's Mystery Machine*. Adapted and reprinted from *Mario's Mystery Machine*, Text © 1972 by Sibyl Hancock, by permission of the author, originally published by G. P. Putnam's Sons.

Harper & Row, Publishers Inc. for the adaptation of *Chameleon Was A Spy* (text only) by Diane Redfield Massie (Thomas Y. Crowell). Copyright © 1974 by Diane Redfield Massie. Also for the adaptation of the text of *The Troll Music* by Anita Lobel. Copyright © 1966 by Anita Lobel. Both reprinted by permission of Harper & Row, Publishers, Inc.

The Putnam Publishing Group for *Nate The Great And The Lost List* by Marjorie Weinman Sharmat. Adapted and reprinted by permission of Coward, McCann & Geoghegan, Inc., from *Nate The Great And The Lost List*, text © 1975 by Marjorie Weinman Sharmat, illustrations © 1975 by Marc Simont.

Random House, Inc. for the adaptation from *The Surprise Party*, by Annabelle Prager. Copyright © 1977 by Annabelle Prager. Reprinted by permission of Pantheon Books, a Division of Random House, Inc.

Marian Reiner for the poem "Whispers" from *Whispers and Other Poems* by Myra Cohn Livingston. Copyright © 1958 by Myra Cohn Livingston. Reprinted by permission of Marian Reiner for the author.

Contents

Inventions

Maybe if I move this wheel over there . . .
     Yes, but then that gear won't work . . .
How about adding a gear
     that turns the other way . . .
     But then the propeller won't fit . . .
Suppose I put this over here . . .
     And then . . .
Hurray!!
     It works!!

The Marvellous Toy

By Tom Paxton

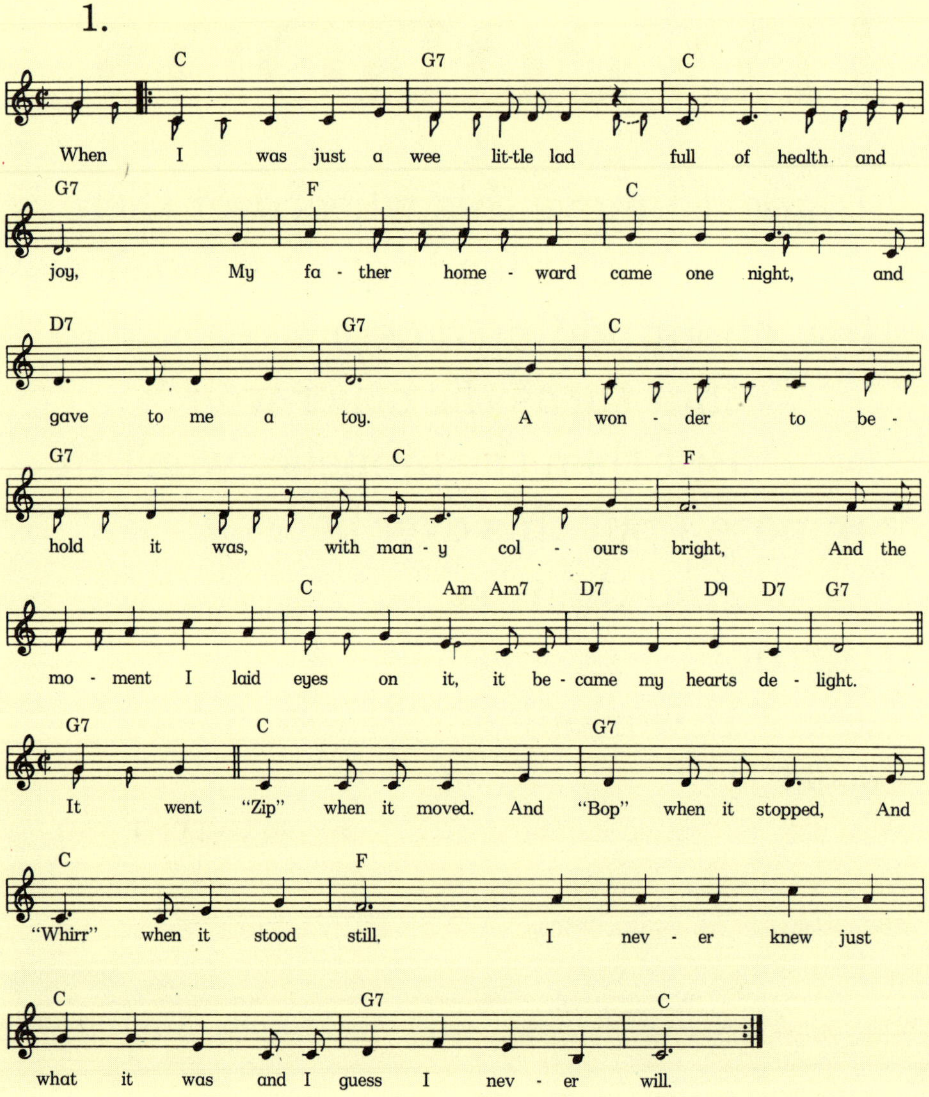
1.
C G7 C
When I was just a wee lit-tle lad full of health and
G7 F C
joy, My fa - ther home - ward came one night, and
D7 G7 C
gave to me a toy. A won - der to be -
G7 C F
hold it was, with man - y col - ours bright, And the
C Am Am7 D7 D9 D7 G7
mo - ment I laid eyes on it, it be - came my hearts de - light.
G7 C G7
It went "Zip" when it moved. And "Bop" when it stopped, And
C F
"Whirr" when it stood still. I nev - er knew just
C G7 C
what it was and I guess I nev - er will.

2.

The first time that I picked it up, I had a big surprise
For right on its bottom were two big buttons that
looked like big green eyes.
I first pushed one, then the other, then I twisted its lid
And when I set it down again, here is what it did.
It went "Zip" when it moved, "Bop" when it stopped,
"Whirr" when it stood still.
I never knew just what it was, and I guess I never will.

3.

It first marched left, then marched right, then
marched under a chair,
And when I looked where it had gone, it wasn't even
there.
I started to cry, my daddy laughed, for he knew that
I would find
When I turned around, my marvellous toy chuggin'
from behind.
It went "Zip" when it moved, "Bop" when it stopped,
"Whirr" when it stood still.
I never knew just what it was, and I guess I never will.

Mario's Mystery Machine

By Sibyl Hancock
Illustrated by Maureen Shaughnessy

Mario stood on his porch in the warm sunshine. He smiled and said to himself, "In all the world there can be no one with a better secret than mine!"

Then Mario went off into town.

He rang the bell at the hardware store. "Good morning! I would like to buy some tools."

"Tools?" said the hardware man. "Why? What would you do with tools?"

Mario said nothing. But under his big hat he hid a wide smile.

Back to his house Mario went and got out his tools. He closed his curtains and went to work. The tools clanged and banged and pounded and buzzed.

The clatter was so loud that people came out into the streets.

"What is happening in Mario's house?" they asked. But not one of them knew the secret.

"I'll find out what Mario is doing," said the hardware man.

He marched up and knocked on the door.

"Mario!" he said. "What is it you are making?"

"Come in and see for yourself," said Mario.

But all the hardware man saw was something tall and wide that was covered with a sheet.

"You may have a peep," Mario said, and he slowly lifted one part of the sheet.

"A machine?" the hardware man cried. "What does it do?"

"Ah," Mario said, "you must wait and see." And that was all he would say.

The more Mario worked, the bigger the machine grew. "My machine will be magnificent!" he cried.

The crowd in Mario's garden grew larger and larger.

"What will the machine do?" the people asked one another.

The barber was worried. "This machine will ruin me. It is a hair-cutting machine and will do my job!"

"No, no!" said the baker. "It will be a cake maker, a tart baker, a cutter of biscuits!"

"What about me?" the greengrocer asked. "That terrible machine will make food!"

Never had a little town had such a mystery! And never had Mario worked so hard! The machine got bigger and bigger and noisier and noisier.

Then one day Mario opened his door and put up a sign. It said:

Tomorrow!

Grand Opening!

And the next day all the worried people came—the greengrocer, the baker, the barber, the hardware man, and all the rest. They came to learn what the machine did.

"Watch!" Mario cried. And with one hand he pulled off the sheet that covered his magnificent machine. Then he threw a switch, and the machine began to move.

Never had anyone in the town seen such a sight!

Toy trains choo-chooed over mountains. Whistles tooted, clocks spun, and chimneys puffed. Red lights blinked, and birds sang.

The barber began to laugh and the baker said, "The machine does *nothing*!"

"Nothing!" cried Mario. "You say it does *nothing*? It does what no other machine will ever do. It makes laughter! It makes you laugh, my friends!"

The people smiled; then they giggled; then they laughed; then they roared! Mario's house was full of laughter.

Today the little town is known far and wide for its happy people. Whenever people feel sad, they go to Mario's house and watch toy trains choo-chooing over mountains, whistles tooting, clocks spinning, chimneys puffing, red lights blinking, and birds singing.

And who is the happiest man of them all? Who but the magnificent Mario!

Everyday Inventions

Illustrated by Joan Affleck

Everything that you use every day was once invented by someone. Think about that for a while. The book you are reading, the desk you are sitting in, the clothes you are wearing, the pencil you wrote with today, the cereal you had for breakfast—the list goes on and on.

Some of these things were thought of by inventors and scientists. Others were invented by people like you.

The Toothbrush

How would you clean your teeth if there were no toothbrushes?

Long ago people used rags to do this job. Then one morning about two hundred years ago, William Addis had a good idea. He took a piece of bone and made lots of little holes at one end of it. Then he cut some brush bristles and stuck these into the holes with glue. That's how the toothbrush was invented.

Jigsaw Puzzles

A teacher named John Spilsbury invented jigsaw puzzles. He made a map of England and Wales out of wood. Then he sawed it into many pieces. His class had fun putting the pieces of the map together.

The biggest jigsaw puzzle in the world has 40,000 pieces. How long do you think it would take to put it together?

Money

Before metal coins and paper notes were used as money, people paid for things in other ways. Salt was used as money by many people long ago. Whale teeth, shells, iron bars, and even butter were used as money.

Aren't you glad someone thought of using coins and notes?

The Bicycle

Some things were invented and re-invented time after time. Each time they were made better. The bicycle is an invention like this.

A long, long time ago, people rode bicycles. These bicycles had little wheels. To make them go, people had to push along the ground with their feet.

Then in 1816 came the invention of a wooden bicycle that could be steered. In 1839 a bicycle with pedals was invented.

Later bicycles had huge front wheels and small back wheels. Rubber tyres were invented to make bicycles easier to ride.

Finally in 1870 Harry J. Lawson invented a bicycle with a chain drive. This bicycle was very much like the bicycles of today.

But inventors are still working on the bicycle, trying to make it faster and better. What changes would you make to bicycles?

You Can Be an Inventor, Too

Illustrated by Joan Affleck

Inventors are people who look at problems and try to think of ways to solve these problems.

Frances Allen wanted to help people who were travelling and had no way to take a bath. She invented the portable bathtub.

Think about some of the problems you have. Does your dog get tangled every time you tie him up outside? Do birds eat the plants in your garden as soon as they come through the ground? Does someone at your house have a hard time getting up every morning? Do you get an itchy spot on your back that you can't reach?

Use your imagination to invent something to solve one of your problems. Be sure to try out your invention to see if it works!

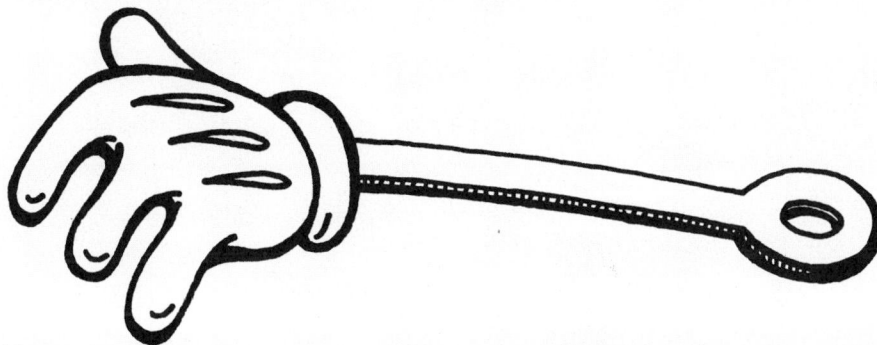

Nate the Great and the Lost List

By Marjorie Weinman Sharmat
Illustrated by Marc Simont

Part One

I, Nate the Great, am a busy detective. One morning I was not busy. I was on my holiday. I was sitting under a tree with my dog, Sludge, and a pancake. Sludge needed a holiday, too.

My friend Claude came into the garden. I knew that he had lost something. That's the way Claude was.

"I lost my way to your house," he said. "And then I found it."

"What else did you lose?" I asked.

"I lost the list I was taking to the shop. Can you help me find it?"

"I, Nate the Great, am on my holiday," I said.

"When will your holiday be over?"

"At lunch," I answered.

"I need the list before lunch," Claude said.

"Very well. I, Nate the Great, will take your case. Tell me, what did you have to buy?"

"If I could remember, I wouldn't need the list," Claude said.

"Good thinking," I said.

"Can you remember any of the things on the list?"
I asked.

"Yes," Claude said. "I remember salt, milk, butter, flour, sugar, and tuna-fish."

"Now tell me," I said, "where did you lose the list?"

"If I knew, I could find it," Claude said.

"You can't be sure of that," I said. "What streets did you walk on?"

"I'm not sure," Claude said. "I lost my way a few times."

"Then I, Nate the Great, know what to do," I said. "I will draw a map. It will have every street between your house and the shop. We will look there."

Sludge and I got up. Our holiday was over.

I got a piece of paper and made a map.

Claude said, "I will walk with you."

We walked between Claude's house and the shop. Then we walked between the shop and Claude's house. Sludge sniffed, but we could not find the list.

"Maybe it blew away," I said. I dropped the map to the ground.

"What are you doing?" Claude asked.

"I dropped the map," I answered. "The way it goes will show us which way the wind is blowing. Maybe we will learn where your list blew."

The map blew over to Rosa's house.

"I will go to Rosa's house," I said. "I will ask her if she has seen your list."

Sludge and I went to Rosa's house. Rosa opened the door. She looked strange and white. She was covered with flour. Sludge sniffed hard. I sniffed hard. Rosa smelled great. She was making pancakes!

We walked in. Rosa's four black cats were there. Today they were white, too.

"I am making cat pancakes from a new recipe," Rosa said. "I am having a cat pancake party this morning."

"I would like to taste cat pancakes," I said.

"You are not a cat," Rosa said.

"I would like to taste them anyway," I said. "A pancake is a pancake."

Rosa and I sat down. I ate a pancake. It had a fishy taste. I ate another. It tasted even more fishy.

"I am looking for Claude's shopping list," I said. "I think the wind blew it to your house. Have you seen it?"

"I haven't seen a shopping list," Rosa said.

I got up. "Thank you for your help and your pancakes." I said.

Part Two

Sludge and I walked to Claude's house. Claude was home. He was not lost. It was a good sign.

"I, Nate the Great, have not found your list," I said. "Can you remember anything else you had to buy?"

"How will that help you find the list?" Claude asked.

"You'll see," I said.

"I remember! I remember two more things," Claude said. "Eggs and baking powder were on the list."

"Very good," I said.

"Can you find the list before lunch?" Claude asked.

"I hope so," I said. "Come to my house around twelve."

Sludge and I walked home slowly.
This was a hard case.

At home I made myself some pancakes. I mixed eggs, flour, salt, baking powder, milk, butter, and sugar together. Then I cooked them.

I gave Sludge a bone. I ate and thought. I thought about the shopping list. I thought about Rosa and her fishy cat pancakes. I put ideas together. I took them apart.

Then I had a big idea. I knew I must go back to Rosa's house.

Sludge and I walked quickly to Rosa's house. I said hello to Rosa and to more cats than I could count.

"I came to talk about your cat pancakes," I said.

"Would you like more?" Rosa asked.

"I would like to see your recipe," I said.

"Here it is," Rosa said.

"Tell me, where did you get this recipe?" I asked.

"I found it today!" Rosa said.

"You found it? Did you find it near your house?" I asked.

"Yes," Rosa said. "How did you know that?"

"I have something to tell you," I said. "I, Nate the Great, say that your cat pancake recipe is Claude's shopping list."

I read the recipe.

"Salt. Milk. Butter. Flour. Tuna-fish. Eggs. Baking powder. Sugar. Salmon. Liver."

"Oh," Rosa said. "When I found the paper, I thought it was a cat pancake recipe."

"Yes," I said. "When you saw the list, you thought it was what you wanted. You wanted a cat pancake recipe."

"I, Nate the Great, solved the case when I was making pancakes," I said. "I mixed eggs, flour, salt, baking powder, milk, butter, and sugar. Claude had told me they were on his list. The other thing he remembered he had to buy was tuna-fish. Cats like tuna-fish. So, I came up with cat pancakes!"

"Oh," Rosa said. "Well, Claude can have his paper back. I will keep the recipe in my head."

"That is a good place for it," I said. "It cannot blow away."

Sludge and I went home with the list. The case was solved.

It is now after twelve. Here comes Claude. I am glad the case is over. I, Nate the Great, have something important to do.

I, Nate the Great, am going to go back to my holiday.

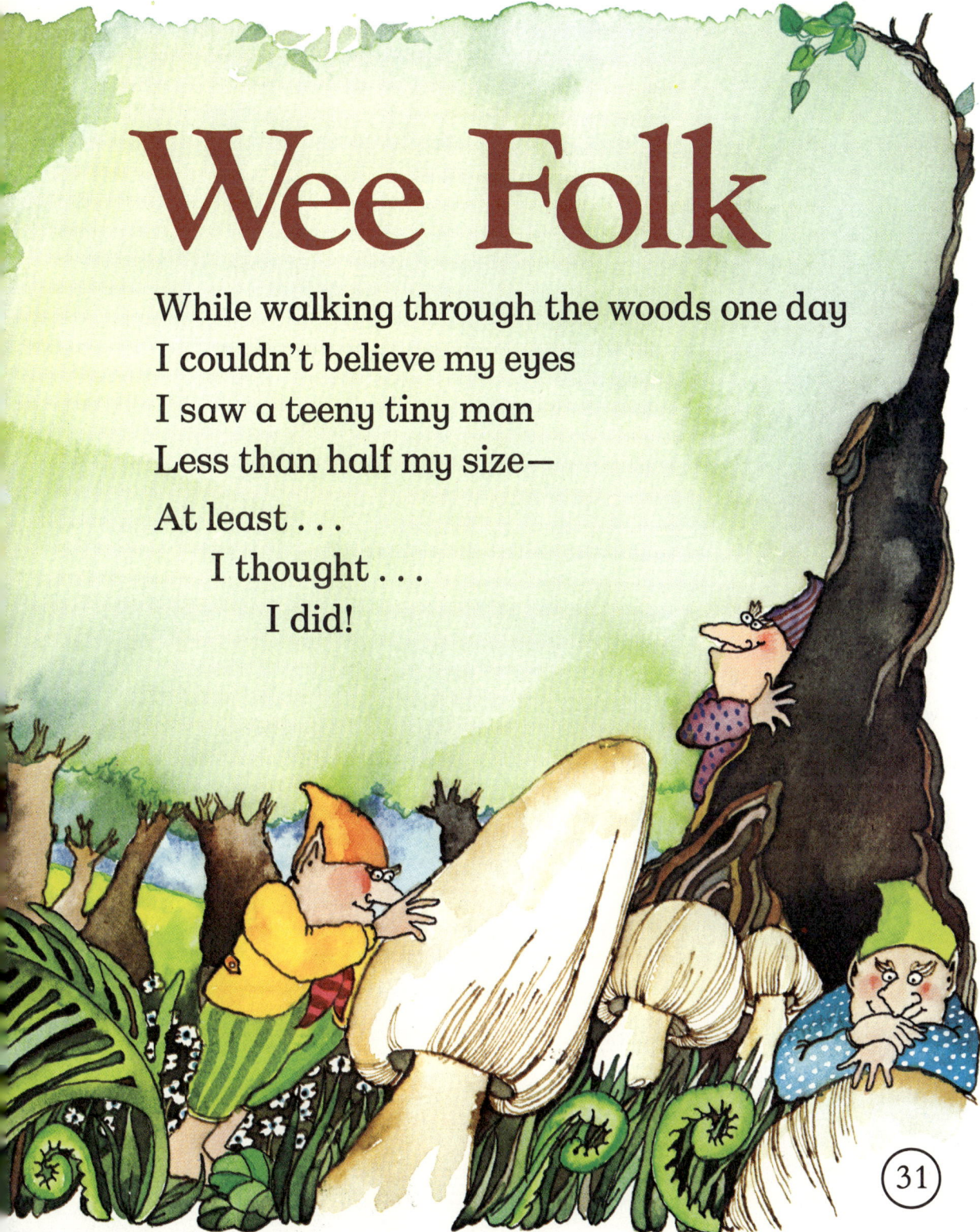

Wee Folk

While walking through the woods one day
I couldn't believe my eyes
I saw a teeny tiny man
Less than half my size—

At least . . .
    I thought . . .
        I did!

The Teeny Tiny Woman

Illustrated by Tina Holdcroft

Once upon a time, there was a teeny tiny woman who lived in a teeny tiny house.

One day this teeny tiny woman put on her teeny tiny hat and went out of her teeny tiny house to take a teeny tiny walk.

When the teeny tiny woman had gone a teeny tiny way, she came to a teeny tiny gate. So the teeny tiny woman opened the teeny tiny gate and went into a teeny tiny field.

In the teeny tiny field, the teeny tiny woman found a teeny tiny bone. She said to her teeny tiny self, "This teeny tiny bone will make me some teeny tiny soup for my teeny tiny supper."

The teeny tiny woman put the teeny tiny bone into her teeny tiny basket and went home to her teeny tiny house.

When the teeny tiny woman got home to her teeny tiny house, she was a teeny tiny bit tired. She put the teeny tiny bone into a teeny tiny cupboard and went up the teeny tiny stairs to her teeny tiny bed.

The teeny tiny woman had been sleeping a teeny tiny time when she was awakened by a teeny tiny voice that came from the teeny tiny cupboard and said, "Give me my bone!"

This made the teeny tiny woman a teeny tiny bit frightened, so she hid her teeny tiny head under her teeny tiny covers and went to sleep again.

And when she had been sleeping a teeny tiny time, the teeny tiny voice in the teeny tiny cupboard called out again a teeny tiny bit louder,
"Give me my bone!"

This made the teeny tiny woman a teeny tiny bit more frightened, so she hid her teeny tiny head a teeny tiny bit farther under her teeny tiny covers.

And when she had been sleeping again for a teeny tiny time, the teeny tiny voice in the teeny tiny cupboard said a teeny tiny bit louder,
"GIVE ME MY BONE!"

Now the teeny tiny woman was a teeny tiny bit more frightened, but she stuck her teeny tiny head out of her teeny tiny covers and said in her loudest teeny tiny voice,
"TAKE IT!"

Anything

By Heather Halpern
Illustrated by Marilyn Mets

When I sit upon the floor
I can go to a sunny shore.
I can be a king or queen,
I can be a dragon mean.
I can be a tiny elf
Under a toadstool by myself.

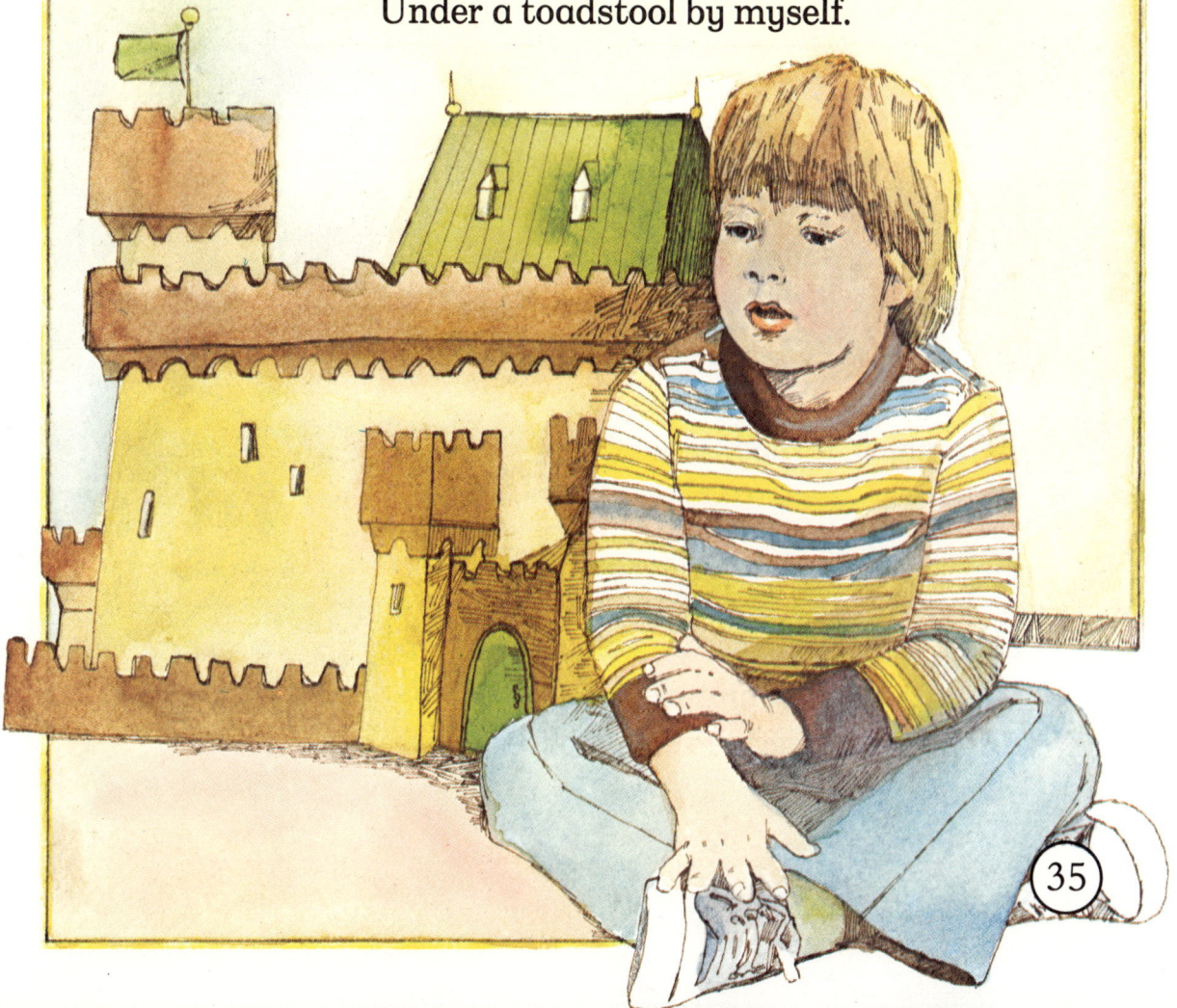

All about Elves

Illustrated by Frank Hammond

Long ago, many people all over the world believed in small people called elves or fairies. Sometimes these imaginary creatures were helpful to people, but more often they were mischievous. People thought they had magic powers and could cast spells. Many stories were told about these little people.

Pixies

In the stories, pixies were pretty, little people who always dressed in green clothes. They loved to dance and play tunes on bells. Pixies also liked to play tricks. When people got lost, they used to blame pixies.

Goblins

Goblins in the stories were small, nasty elves. Some of them could turn into animals. Hallowe'en was the time when goblins liked to be out.

Leprechauns

Leprechauns were little old men who made shoes. People believed that leprechauns were very rich. If you caught a leprechaun, you would try to make him lead you to his secret pot of gold.

Trolls

Trolls lived in caves or under hills in fine houses made of glass and gold. They could do all kinds of magic. You could tell a troll by his grey jacket and pointed red cap.

Brownies

Brownies were shaggy men who wore ragged, brown clothes. They were about one metre tall. Brownies picked one house to live in, and they always worked hard at night helping the people there. To thank the brownies, people left out a bowl of milk and cake with honey.

The Troll Music

By Anita Lobel
Illustrated by Deborah Drew-Brook-Cormack

Once there was a band of musicians who woke with the sun and went marching through the countryside playing music all day long. There was a tuba player, a trombone player, a cello player, a trumpet player, and a little boy who played the flute.

They played for kings and shoemakers, for ladies and for children. Everyone said that their music was the best in the land.

One evening the musicians fell asleep near a forest. A troll came by and saw the sleeping musicians and their instruments.

"Ah, music, music in the moonlight," he thought. "I could sing and dance, if I heard some music!"

He poked the musicians with a stick and he kicked them. He climbed a tree and shook nuts down on them. But the tired players slept on and on. The troll became angry.

"Wake up! Wake up!" he screamed. "I want music!"

The little flute player woke up just in time to see the troll swish his tail over the musicians, grumble some magic words, and vanish.

In the morning the musicians went to the next town to play.

"Moo-o-o," went the tuba.

"Baa-a-a," went the cello.

"Neigh, neigh," went the trombone.

"Honk, honk," went the trumpet.

"Cluck, cluck, cluck," went the flute.

The people who had come to listen became very angry and threw sticks and stones at the musicians, who fled as fast as they could.

Outside the town gates, the musicians cried, "What has happened to our beautiful music?" Then they tried to play their instruments again.

"Moo-o-o," went the tuba. A cow thought she heard another cow and came across the field to look.

"Baa-a-a," went the cello, and a lamb came looking for a friend.

"Neigh, neigh," went the trombone, and a horse galloped toward them over the grass.

"Honk, honk," went the trumpet, and a goose came to listen to the goose she heard.

"Cluck, cluck, cluck," went the flute, and a little hen came and joined the other animals.

"What shall we do? What shall we do?" cried the musicians. "People will never listen to our music and clap for us again."

"I think I know what to do," the flute player cried. "These animals can help us make some gifts for the troll. We can try to exchange them for our music."

The others were puzzled, but when they saw the flute player hold up an egg the little hen had laid, they began to understand.

The musicians baked a cake. From the lamb's wool they wove some cloth and made a sweater. From the cloth and goose down they made a pillow. The flute player made a wreath of flowers. Then they put everything on the horse's back and went to look for the troll.

Late at night they came to the dark forest. They heard snoring from under a tree and almost fell on a pile of leaves. Three little trolls and a mother troll crawled out.

"Excuse me," said the flute player to Mrs. Troll. "We are looking for Mr. Troll."

An angry voice said, "Let me sleep. I had a busy day!" The troll peeped out from under the leaves.

"We have some good things for you," cried the musicians. "Please take the spell off our music."

"Spell? Have you been running around mumbling magic words again? For shame!" said Mrs. Troll. And she chased Mr. Troll up a tree.

Mrs. Troll looked at all the presents. She sat on the pillow and put on the flower wreath. She tasted the cake. The troll children ate some cake and went for a ride on the horse.

"I want some cake," cried the troll from his tree.

Mrs. Troll went on eating. After a while she said very sweetly, "This might be a real party if we had some music."

"I want some cake," said the troll.

"Take the spell off and you may have some," said Mrs. Troll.

Climbing out of the tree, the troll mumbled some magic words and swished his tail three times at the moon.

The musicians tried their instruments, not knowing what might happen. To their surprise, their music sounded better than ever.

When the animals heard the beautiful music, they began to dance, and everyone else joined in. And they all sang and ate cake and played games. It was a lovely party.

In the morning the musicians woke up, said goodbye to the trolls, and thanked the animals. They picked up their instruments, started playing, and marched out of the forest.

When they came to the next town, the people clapped and cheered. "The musicians are back," someone cried. "And listen! Their music sounds more beautiful than ever!"

And it was true.

The Shoemaker and the Elves

A tale by the Brothers Grimm
Photographed by Derek Case

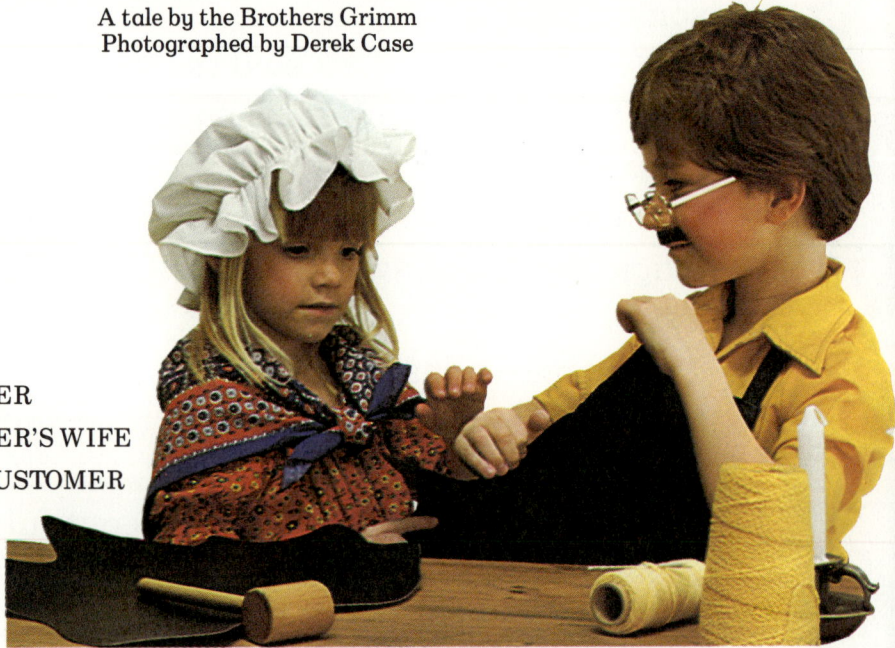

Players

THE SHOEMAKER
THE SHOEMAKER'S WIFE
MR. BLACK, A CUSTOMER
FIRST ELF
SECOND ELF

Act One

STORYTELLER: There was once a hard-working shoemaker. Every day he made fine shoes and sold them to his customers. But he was unlucky in his shop, and he grew poorer and poorer.

SHOEMAKER: Oh me! Oh my! I have only enough leather left to make one pair of shoes. *(The shoemaker holds up a small piece of leather.)*

WIFE: But they will be such fine shoes! *(She pats the shoemaker on the back.)* Don't be sad, husband. I'm sure that some good luck will come our way soon.

SHOEMAKER: Yes, you're right. Tonight I'll cut out this leather, and tomorrow I'll sew the shoes. *(The shoemaker's wife leaves. The shoemaker cuts the leather and lays the pieces out on his work table.)*

SHOEMAKER: *(Yawning.)* There, I've finished. Now I can go to bed. *(The shoemaker goes out. When the clock strikes twelve, two elves in ragged, brown clothes dance into the room. They look at the pieces of leather.)*

FIRST ELF: *(In a high, squeaky voice.)* This shoemaker is a good man, but he's very unlucky. Let's help him.

SECOND ELF: *(In a low voice.)* Yes, we'll sew the finest pair of shoes in the world from this leather.

STORYTELLER: So all through the night, the elves worked and worked. When they were finally finished, just before morning, they put the shoes on the shoemaker's table. The next morning when the shoemaker came down to work on the shoes, he couldn't believe his eyes. *(The shoemaker comes in, yawning and rubbing his eyes.)*

SHOEMAKER: *(Surprised.)* What's this? But how can this be? I didn't make these shoes! Wife, wife, come look! *(The shoemaker's wife comes in. She picks up the shoes and looks at them.)*

WIFE: My, what beautiful shoes! Did you sew them last night?

SHOEMAKER: No, I just cut out the leather. Someone came here in the night and sewed them for me.

WIFE: I wonder who it could have been. *(The door of the shoemaker's shop opens. Mr. Black, a customer, comes in.)*

MR. BLACK: I need a pair of shoes. Could I try these on?

SHOEMAKER: Yes, please do. Sit down. *(Mr. Black sits down and takes off his shoes. The shoemaker helps him put on the new shoes.)*

MR. BLACK: *(He gets up and walks around.)* A perfect fit! What beautiful shoes these are! I'll buy them. Here are four pieces of gold.

SHOEMAKER: *(He looks in surprise at the money in his hand.)* Thank you very much, kind sir! Goodbye. *(Mr. Black leaves.)*

SHOEMAKER: Look, my dear, four pieces of gold! That is enough to buy leather for two pairs of shoes!

STORYTELLER: So the shoemaker bought enough leather for two pairs of shoes. That night he cut out the leather for the shoes, and then he went to bed. The next morning when he came into the shop, there were two beautiful pairs of shoes on his table. He sold these shoes for enough money to buy the leather for four pairs of shoes. And so it went, night after night, day after day. The poor shoemaker was soon poor no longer.

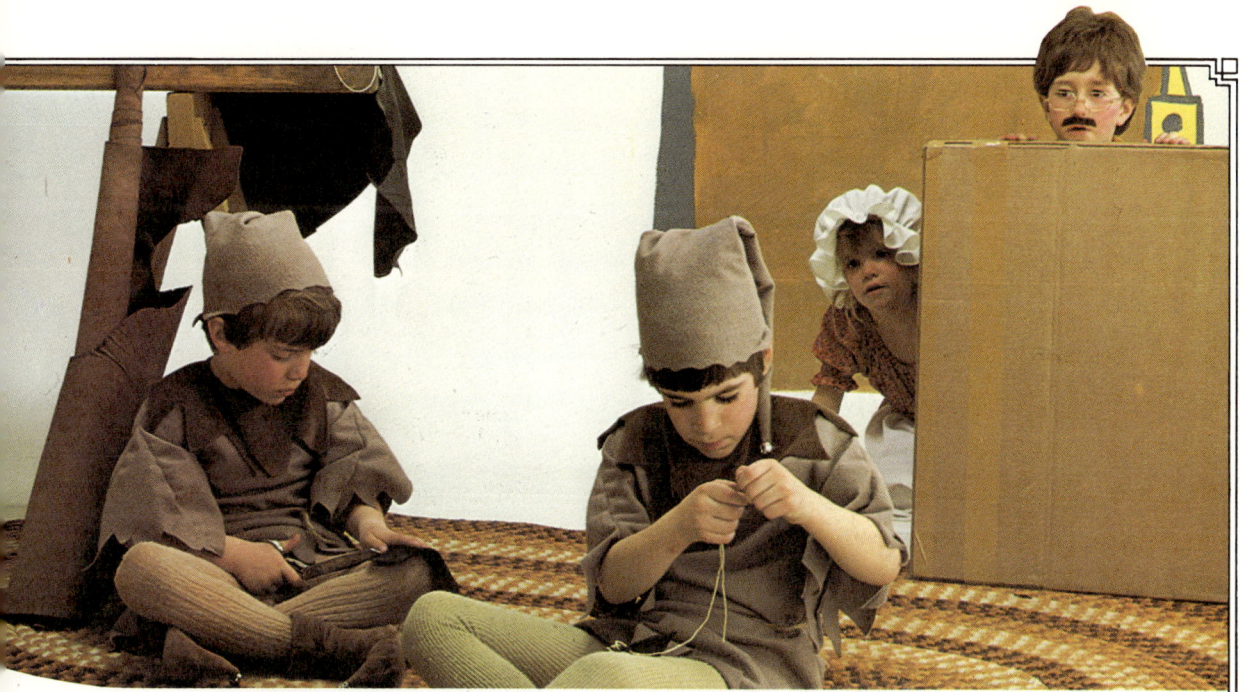

Act Two

STORYTELLER: Finally the shoemaker and his wife decided that they wanted to find out who was sewing the shoes for them. So that night they hid in the work room and waited.

(The shoemaker and his wife hide and wait. When the clock strikes twelve, the two elves in ragged clothes dance into the room and begin to work.)

SHOEMAKER: *(Whispering.)* So these are our helpers!

WIFE: *(Whispering.)* And I know just how we can thank them for all the work they've done for us. *(The next day. The shoemaker and his wife are hard at work making tiny clothes and shoes.)*

WIFE: There, I've finished. I've made each little man a little shirt, a little coat, a little hat, and a little pair of pants.

49

SHOEMAKER: And I've made two little pairs of shoes, one for each of them.

WIFE: Let's lay out the things we've made on the table. They'll soon be here. *(They put the things on the table. Then they hide and wait. When the clock strikes twelve, the two elves skip into the room.)*

FIRST ELF: *(In a high, squeaky voice.)* Look at these beautiful clothes and shoes the shoemaker and his wife have made for us.
(He holds up the coat.)

SECOND ELF: *(In a low voice.)* Let's put them on. *(The elves put on the clothes and shoes. They run to look in the mirror in the shop.)*

FIRST ELF: *(Clapping his hands.)* We look so handsome!

BOTH ELVES: *(Chanting.)*

What spruce and dandy boys are we!

No longer cobblers will we be.

(The two elves skip out of the room.

The shoemaker and his wife come out of hiding.)

WIFE: I'm so glad that they liked their presents.

SHOEMAKER: Yes, everything was a perfect fit.

STORYTELLER: After that night the elves never came back to the shop. But the luck that the elves gave to the shoemaker and his wife lasted, and they were never poor again.

I Know Something You Don't Know

Whispers
> tickle through your ear
> telling things you like to hear.

Whispers
> are as soft as skin
> letting little words curl in.

Whispers
> come so they can blow
> secrets others never know.

By Myra Cohn Livingston

53

Secret Favour Day

By Elizabeth Bram
Illustrated by Lisa Smith

One day when Woodruff was walking down the street, he saw Mrs. Flagg's hat blow off. It blew so far away that by the time he caught it, Mrs. Flagg was gone.

Woodruff took the hat back to her house and left it on the front porch. Then he waited behind a bush until she came out and found it.

Mrs. Flagg was surprised and happy. Woodruff was excited. He decided to spend the whole afternoon doing secret favours for people.

It was not hard to find favours to do.

As soon as he left Mrs. Flagg's house, he met Mr. Stewart's dog, Sam, who was loose again. Woodruff took him back home before he was even missed. Then he replanted some flowers that Sam had dug up.

Next he put a coin in a parking meter just before the traffic warden came by to put a ticket on the car.

"This is fun," said Woodruff. "What else can I do?"

As he stood and wondered, the paper-girl rode by on her bike. She tossed a newspaper at every house. But some of the papers fell into bushes. Woodruff found the newspapers and put them next to each front door.

He moved a toy wagon out of Mr. White's drive so he would not drive over it. Then he moved a roller-skate away from the front path.

And then Woodruff went home.

"I've been looking for you," said his mother. "Where have you been?"

"Out," said Woodruff.

"What were you doing all afternoon?"

"I was busy. It's a secret favour day," said Woodruff.

"Were you the one who took back Mrs. Flagg's hat?" asked his mother.

"I can't tell you," said Woodruff. "It's a secret."

The Surprise Party

By Annabelle Prager
Illustrated by Barbara Reid

Part One

"Know what?" said Nicky.

"No, what?" said Albert.

"My birthday is coming," said Nicky. "I'm going to have a birthday party."

"Great!" said Albert. "I love birthday parties!"

"Come on. I need you to help me," said Nicky.

Nicky took out his money-box. He shook it upside down. Out fell two coins.

"Oh, no!" he said. "This isn't enough for a party."

"What are you going to do?" asked Albert.

"I'll think of something," said Nicky.
Then he smiled.

"I know," he said. "I'll have a surprise party."

"A surprise party for who?" asked Albert.

"A surprise party for me," said Nicky.

"You can't give a surprise party for yourself," said Albert. "You won't be surprised."

"I know I can't give a surprise party for myself," said Nicky. "But *you* can. You and Ann, and Jenny and Jan, and Morris and Doris, and Dan can give the party."

"How are we going to do that?" asked Albert.

"Easy," said Nicky. "You'll say—'Nicky's birthday is coming. Let's give him a surprise party'. Then they'll say—'What a good idea! We love surprise parties'. One person can bring paper plates, another can bring a cake..."

"Oh, I get it," said Albert. "Everyone will bring something for the party. What a good idea."

"You can get the party ready at my house while I am out having my tuba lesson," Nicky said. "When I come home, you will yell SURPRISE! I'll be surprised if this isn't the best surprise party ever."

Albert ran home. He called up Ann, and Jenny and Jan, and Morris and Doris, and Dan. Sure enough, they all said, "What a good idea! We love surprise parties."

They all met at Albert's house to plan the party.

"We can get the party ready at Nicky's house while he is out having his tuba lesson," Albert said. "When he comes home, we will yell SURPRISE!"

Just then the telephone rang. Albert answered it. "Hello," he said.

It was Nicky. "I forgot to tell you something," said Nicky. "I love balloons with Happy Birthday on them."

"OK," said Albert. "Goodbye."

"Who was that?" asked Ann.

Albert thought very fast. "That was my Aunt Betsy," he said. "Shall we have balloons with Happy Birthday on them?"

"Yes, yes, yes," shouted everyone.

The telephone rang again.

"I forgot something else," said Nicky. "I love the colour blue."

"Oh, yes, Aunt Betsy," said Albert. "Goodbye!"

"Why does your aunt call you all the time?" asked Morris and Doris.

"My Aunt Betsy likes me," said Albert.

"Now let me think. Nicky loves the colour blue. Shall I make a beautiful blue birthday cake?"

"Oh, yes! Nicky will be surprised!" everyone said.

Part Two

The next day Nicky and Albert went out for a walk.

"It wouldn't be good if the others found out that I know about the party!" said Nicky.

"Sh-h-h," said Albert. "Here comes Ann."

"I'll make sure that Ann doesn't think I know about the party," said Nicky.

"Hello," said Ann.

"Hello, Ann," said Nicky. "Do you know what I am doing on my birthday?"

"What?" asked Ann.

"My tuba teacher is taking me to a concert," said Nicky.

"Oh, no," said Ann.

"Why do you say 'Oh, no'?" asked Nicky.

"What I wanted to say," said Ann, "was, Oh, no kidding? Well, now I have to go to see Jenny and Jan, and Morris and Doris, and Dan. Goodbye."

Nicky laughed. "I fooled her," he said. "Now nobody can think that I know about the party. Oh, I can't wait for my birthday to come!"

Nicky was walking home from his tuba lesson. He gave a little hop. His birthday had come at last. When Nicky got to his house, it was all dark. He practised making a surprised face. He opened his front door. Nothing happened.

He went into the front room. Nothing happened. He turned on the light. Nobody was there.

"Where's the party?" he asked himself. "They must be hiding." Nicky waited and waited. Nothing happened.

Then the doorbell rang.

"There they are!" Nicky thought. He practised making a few surprised faces on the way to the door.

It was Albert, all by himself.

"Where's my party?" asked Nicky.

"Oh, Nicky," said Albert, "it's too bad. Ann told everyone that you were going to a concert with your tuba teacher. They called off the party."

"Oh, why did I play a trick on my friends?" cried Nicky.

"Don't be too sad," said Albert. "They decided to have the party on your next birthday. You can think about it for a whole year. But I made a cake for you anyway. It's at my house."

They walked to Albert's house. Albert opened his front door. Nicky went in. Albert turned on the light.

"Surprise! Surprise!" shouted Ann, and Jenny and Jan, and Morris and Doris, and Dan.

Nicky looked all around him. There were balloons with Happy Birthday on them. In the middle of the table there was a beautiful blue birthday cake. By each blue paper plate, there was a blue cracker. Best of all, there was a big pile of presents. Each one had a surprise inside.

"Wow!" said Nicky.

"Know what?" said Albert.

"No, what?" said Nicky.

"You said you wanted the best surprise party that ever was," said Albert. "So we made it a real surprise."

My Box

By Myra Cohn Livingston
Photographed by Derek Case

Nobody knows what's there but me,
knows where I keep my silver key
and my playing cards
and my water gun
and my wind-up car that doesn't run,
and a stone I found with a hole clear through
and an old jay feather that's *mostly* blue,
. . . important things that I'll never show
to anyone, *anyone* else I know.

Keeping Secrets

Some people have secret boxes where they keep special things. Some people have books where they write secrets. Some people have secret places where they like to go. Do you have any secrets like these?

Some secrets are fun because you are the only one who knows them. Other secrets are fun because you can share them with a friend.

One way to share secrets is to send secret messages to your friends. You can write a secret message with invisible ink. Write your words with a toothpick, using lemon juice or milk for ink. To read the message, hold the paper above a hot light bulb. After a while you will see the words.

Another way of sending a secret message is by writing words in code. You can find books of codes in your library.

You can also use a special language like Pig Latin to share secrets with a friend. The Pig Latin message, *idehay hetay oxbay*, says, *hide the box*. Can you see how Pig Latin works?

Chameleon Was a Spy

Adapted from Chameleon Was a Spy
By Diane Redfield Massie
Re-illustrated by Tina Holdcroft

Part One

Chameleon liked to change colours. He could match the rug and the chair. He could match the walls and the curtains.

"I can match anything," said Chameleon. "You name it."

It was even hard for his mother to find him. "Chameleon!" she would call, standing right next to him. "Where are you?"

"I will be a spy when I grow up," said Chameleon. "No one will ever catch me."

One day, as he was reading the paper, he saw a small advertisement. "WANTED," it said, "SOMEONE FOR SUPER SECRET WORK. Apply at: Number 222 South Bean Street."

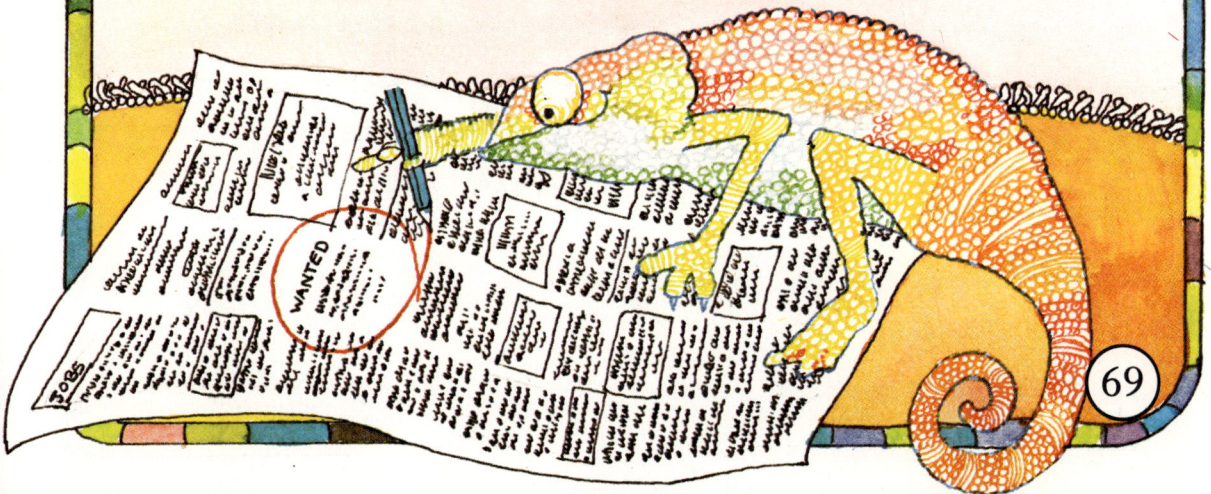

"I'm going to get a job," Chameleon told his mother.

"Good luck," said his mother.

Chameleon went to the city to Number 222 South Bean Street. It was the Pleasant Pickle Company.

Chameleon knocked.

"Who's there?" said a voice.

"It's Chameleon," said Chameleon, turning as brown as the door.

"Where? I don't see anyone!" said a man, looking out.

"I'm right here," said Chameleon.

"Oh! A frog!" said the man.

"I'm not a frog," said Chameleon. "I'm a chameleon, and I'm here about the job."

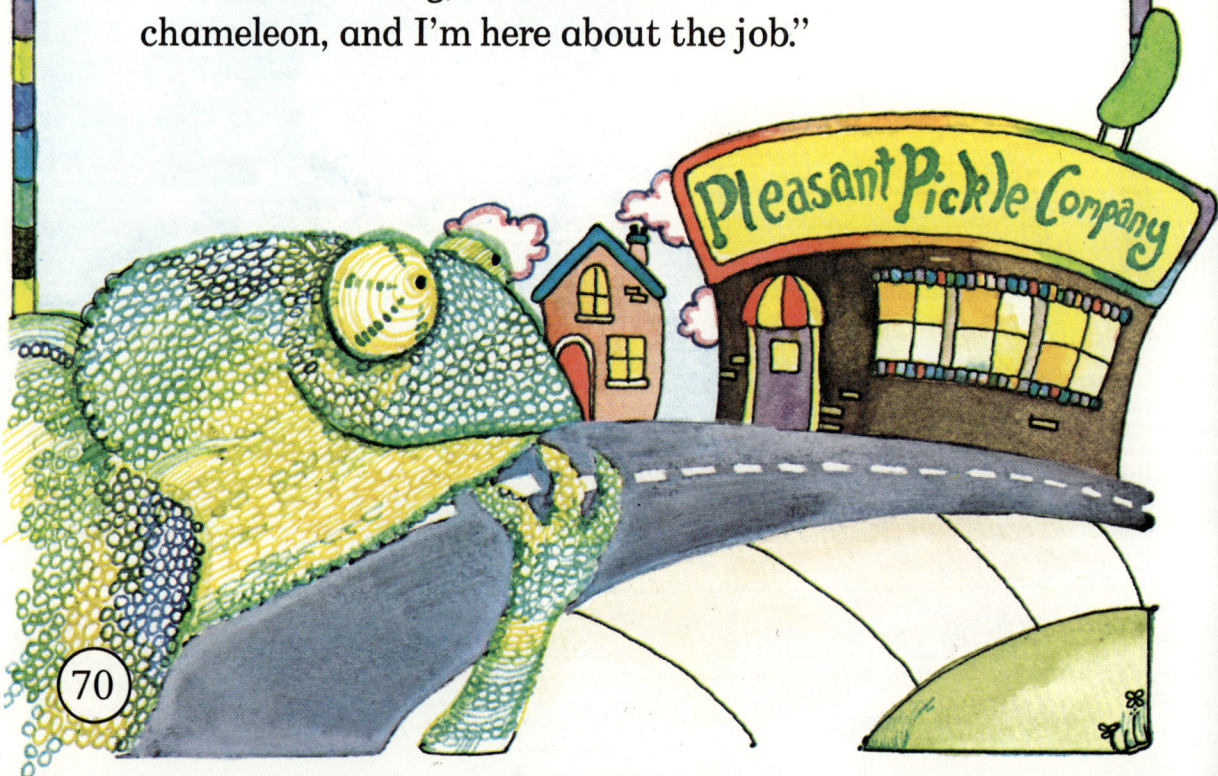

"Follow me," said the man.

Chameleon followed him to a big room.

"Gentlemen," said the man to nine other men who sat around a long table. "This is Mr. Chameleon. He's here about the super secret job."

Everyone looked at Chameleon.

"What kind of work is it anyway?" asked Chameleon.

"Spying," said the Chairman.

"Wow!" said Chameleon.

"Pleasant Pickles have always been the best!" said the Chairman. "But *now* the Perfect Pickle Company will make *better* pickles than we do. They have stolen our secret formula!"

"A pickle scientist took it," said another man. "He works for the Perfect Pickle Company."

"I'll get your formula back," said Chameleon as he leaped onto a plant. He turned as green as a leaf.

"Where is he?" asked the men.

"Here I am!" said Chameleon. He leaped back to the table again. "What do you say?"

"Incredible!" cried the Chairman.

"You're hired!"

Part Two

The next day Chameleon went to the Perfect Pickle Company.

"Laboratories" said a sign on a door.

"This must be where they make the formula," said Chameleon.

Soon a scientist in a long white coat came in.

"Now that I have the Pleasant Pickle formula," he said, "Pleasant Pickles will soon go out of business! Hee, hee!" And he threw the formula on the table.

SECRET
10 kg cucumbers
(soaked in salty brine)
1 large horseradish
8 L vinegar
8 celery seeds
4 dill blossoms
and 250 ml mustard, made with crinkleroot juice
SECRET

Chameleon slid across the table to the formula. "What's this?" said the scientist.

Chameleon slid onto the paper and lay still. His skin matched the words under him. "Crinkleroot juice," they said.

"Wait!" snapped the scientist. His hand grabbed Chameleon and held him by the tail. "You were reading the secret formula! You are a spy!"

Chameleon twisted away and leaped onto the table. He grabbed the secret formula and jumped down to the floor.

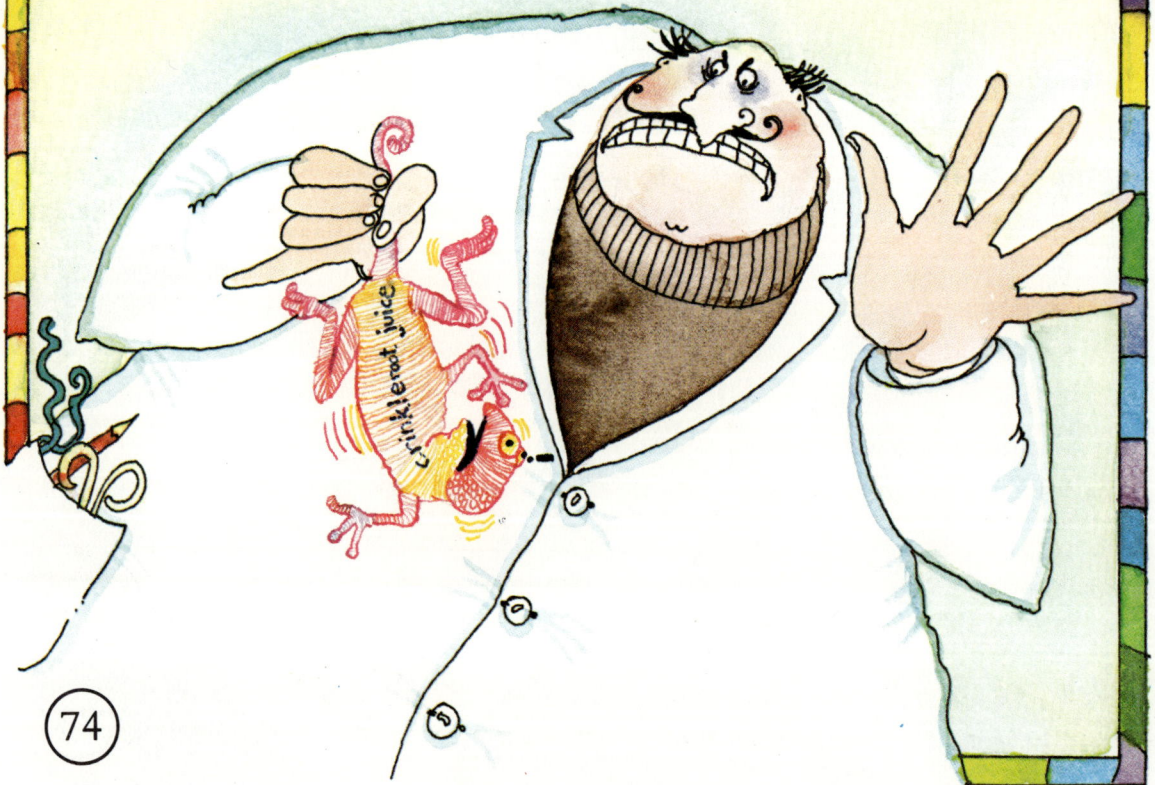

Chameleon ran down the hall. The door at the end said "Pickling Plant."

There were tubs of pickles everywhere.

Bottles were passing under a chute which filled them up with pickles.

"Stop him!" yelled the scientist, rushing through the door.

Chameleon leaped to the pickle chute. But his foot slipped. Down he fell, plunk, into a bottle. Pickles poured down the pickle chute on top of him.

"Help!" yelled Chameleon. But no one heard him. His bottle went into a box with eleven other bottles.

After a very long time, Chameleon felt himself being moved somewhere. Thump! Clunk! Then everything was still.

Part Three

Chameleon opened his eyes. He saw rows and rows of cans and jars. He was in a supermarket.

He waved his arms and pounded on the glass. But no one saw him.

"I'll turn bright red," he said. "*Then* someone's sure to see me."

"Mummy," said a girl, "look at that funny pickle." She picked up Chameleon's jar and put it into her mother's basket.

"Saved at last!" said Chameleon.

The little girl and her mother went to the checkout counter. The cashier picked up Chameleon's jar. Chameleon waved and smiled.

"Eeeeeeeeeeeeeekkkk!" cried the little girl's mother. "What's that?"

The food inspector came. "A contaminated bottle of pickles," he said, "from the Perfect Pickle Company!"

"Let me out!" shouted Chameleon. But no one heard him.

The photographers came from the newspaper. They photographed Chameleon's jar. Then someone took the jar to the police station.

"Perfect Pickle Company Closed!" said the newspapers the next day.

When Chameleon's mother saw the newspaper that morning, she hurried to the city.

"Let my son out of that jar!" she said.

The policeman took off the lid.

"Thank you," said Chameleon. He followed his mother out of the door and hurried home.

"How did you like your new job?" said his mother at breakfast.

"It was all right," said Chameleon, "if you're ready to be a pickle."

Then the telephone rang. "I've read the newspaper," said the Chairman of the Pleasant Pickle Company. "Good work!"

"Thank you," said Chameleon.

"Did you get the formula?"

"Yes," said Chameleon. "I'll bring it right over."

When he got to the Pleasant Pickle Company, the board members picked him up and carried him in. "Yahooo!" they shouted.

Chameleon held up the wrinkled paper. "Here is the formula!" he said.

The Chairman looked at the newspaper. "Oh, no!" he shouted. "The writing at the bottom is blurred. The last ingredient is missing!"

"Wait!" cried Chameleon. He grabbed the secret formula and lay across the bottom where the last line had been, and two words showed up. "Crinkleroot juice."

"That's it!" shouted the Chairman. "Chameleon has saved our formula!"

Then he gave Chameleon a plaque. It said:

"For Chameleon, the Perfect Spy, with thanks from the Pleasant Pickle Company, makers of the world's best pickles."

SECRET
10 kg cucumbers
(soaked in salty brine)
1 large horseradish
8 L vinegar
8 celery seeds
4 dill blossoms
and 250 mL mustard, made with

Crinkleroot juice

Journeys
Level Six
See for Myself

ART DIRECTOR/DESIGNER
Hugh Michaelson

TYPESETTING
PFB Art & Type Ltd.

FILM
Colourgraph Reproduction
Systems Inc.

PRINTING
Chorley & Pickersgill Ltd.